# RETIREMENT IS TWICE AS MUCH HUSBAND ON HALF AS MUCH MONEY

Sylvy

ATHENA PRESS

LONDON

RETIREMENT IS TWICE AS MUCH HUSBAND
ON HALF AS MUCH MONEY
Copyright © Sylvy 2003

ISBN  1  932077  51  0

First Published 2003 by
ATHENA PRESS
Queen's House, 2 Holly Road
Twickenham TW1 4EG
United Kingdom

Printed for Athena Press

# RETIREMENT IS
# TWICE AS MUCH HUSBAND
# ON
# HALF AS MUCH MONEY

*Dedicated to Bernie*

*My ever-loving, dutiful, world's*

*Best perspicacious*

*Number one husband, <u>mine</u>*

He sets the table for breakfast, plus he puts the decaf coffee in my cup! Helps me with my book! Makes sandwiches for lunch! Helps me with my book! Makes leftovers into a great dinner and serves it! Helps me with my book! Runs out early in the morning marketing to avoid crowds!

AND

   HAS

      LOTS

         MORE

            TO

               SAY!

                  READ ON…

## Acknowledgements

Thank you all.

Special thanks to my laugh testers. During the writing their response inspired me to write on. They can't wait to read the finished product.

Deep thanks to P.R.G. and spouse.

Here is to you M.N.G.

*Writing is telling what you know.*

Gertrude Stein


I know:

"Retirement is twice as much husband

on half as much money!"

## About the Author:

Cher—one name. Madonna—one name. Why not Sylvy?

Okay! I'm a wife and mother of two sons. A lover of humor. Yes. Humor is our best friend. It is the *best* prescription for health and happiness. In living the retired life I saw humor in everyday events. Good for the soul.

So I said to myself, "Hey, Sylvy, why not share this humor with all people in the world of retirement and future retirees?"

Thus was born *Retirement is Twice as Much Husband on Half as Much Money.* Read on and learn more about Sylvy. Enjoy hefty, hearty laughs. And these hearty laughs could be sexual. How about that?


Feels good, doesn't it?

Have fun!

# *Preface*

*Retirement Is Twice As Much Husband On Half As Much Money* is original, concise, flavors the reality of retirement with true humorous narratives and hilarious anecdotes, a blend of sads and glads. The retiree can love, remarry, work, create, be productive and remain healthy and happy well into the nineties and beyond with fun, happiness and laughter in their lives.

My book, with humor, captures the reality of husband and wife in a new environment. I rack my brain, trying to remember our marital vows. "YES", for better or worse, in sickness and in health. But, oh, GOD! "NO", not for twenty-four hours a day, seven days a week, three hundred and sixty five days a year; bonus, one extra day every leap year.

The book brings you through the process of selling our home, the trip to Florida, adjustments to new surroundings, new people, a new way of life, and yes, togetherness.

I love you dear husband – but! Strip away the retirement stereotype. We of the retirement age are no longer known as senior citizens. We are grown-ups who are growing younger. The rocking chair has been replaced by the sports car, convertible or motor cycle. The growing younger syndrome is topical, now and forever, with mass appeal.

*Retirement Is Twice As Much Husband On Half As Much Money* merrily invites you to jump into the pool of life and soak in health and happiness.

See you in condo-ville.

# Thirst For Youth

History tells us Juan Ponce de Leon's claim to fame was the quest for the elusive Fountain of Youth in the year 1512.

The search for the Fountain of Youth continues as the endless stream of couples head south, or west, high on retirement, convinced the fountain has been renamed condo-ville.

We looked back, for the last time, as my husband drove away from the house, no longer our home. He took my hand, a moment of silence, our tearful eyes met, in unison we sang out "Onward and onward go the party of two," as we headed south. These words turned back the clock for us.

On Sunday, our pre-children days, we used to enjoy a drive viewing the beautiful countryside.

During one of these outings, I put my arm around my husband and sang out, "Onward and onward go the party of two, let's not turn back." This phrase became a ritual with us. After our firstborn, the party was now three; the second, unknowingly, changed the lyrics to party of four. Then once again, after thirty-five years, we were back to "Onward and onward go the party of two." Young in heart, thinning hair (his), expanding waist (his), graying hair (mine), still pretty shapely (me), optimistic and happy, (both of us), we were rolling along.

Two hundred years ago, give or take a few, when the migration westward started, the pioneers had horse-drawn covered wagons. Today, retirees head south, or west, in overloaded station wagons, still depending on horsepower. We paid heed to the warning of the service manager who did a last-minute check on our station wagon.

"Drive carefully and slowly," he advised, "Keep the speed under fifty miles per hour. If you have to make a sudden stop with that load, it will be a disaster."

We listened, adding an extra day to the travel time. Our car was parked under a light every night at the motel, hoping this would deter a theft. At the slightest offbeat noise, I would jump out of bed to see if someone was breaking into the station wagon. I disturbed my husband so many times the first night, he suggested, "Take the sleeping bag and go outside and sleep next to the wagon."

When I protested his snarling suggestion, he countered with, "The pioneers did it. They slept next to their wagons to protect lives and possessions. They survived without a comfortable motel room, color TV, hot and cold running water, shower and soda machines."

"Yeah! But, they didn't know any better," I blurted.

The next day on the road, I said, "Ya' know dear, the pioneers didn't have a bed of roses. They had to contend with all those Indians." I paused, "How did they ever do it?"

He answered, "And I have to contend with the giant trailer-rigs passing me at seventy-five miles per hour. I keep my fingers crossed the suction doesn't blow us off the road right into their trucks."

We reached our condo after three days, exhausted, happy to have arrived safe and sound, looked skyward, hugged each other and thanked the good Lord.

My husband and I stepped out on the screened terrace of our lovely two-bedroom, two-bath condo just in time to view the setting sun casting its magnificent multi-colored rays upon the lake. A delightful breeze drifted through the rooms.

He turned to me and said, "My dear wife, this is the start of something good, the best is yet to be." He kissed me, paused and added, "I'll finally have my own bathroom."

I smiled sweetly, gave him a love tap on the head and answered, "My love, have you forgotten so soon? It's only yours until the guests arrive. You promised to share it with them."

After a few trips to the station wagon, the necessities for nourishment and sleep were unloaded. From complete physical and emotional exhaustion we slept quite well during our first night in the new world.

# Read The Fine Print

Several months before my husband reached his 62nd birthday, he surprised me with the news that he was seriously thinking of taking early retirement.

"We should think about buying a condo in Florida and move there permanently. We've always enjoyed vacationing there. Let's take the plunge," he told me. "I have been doing my financial homework. I'm positive we can afford it. I've been meeting with our accountant and have come to the conclusion that, financially, it's not to our advantage to put off retirement. We'll never make up in pension benefits what we'll lose if we postpone early retirement. Plus, I've just about had it with the cold winters. I'm ready, can we talk?"

"Retirement!" I blurted out, "Oh my gosh, the day you retire will be a day of infamy for me." I laughed heartily. He did not see the humor in that remark. "You are serious," I continued. "We're too young to settle down in one place instead of traveling. I like being a nomad."

"Dear, retirement wouldn't change anything. We'll still do some traveling. But living in Florida will be like a permanent vacation."

"How do you figure that?" I questioned.

So we talked, mostly he talked. I listened with one ear. My mind was wandering.

In the distance I heard his voice – vacation – together – great – two of us.

I was thinking how happy and content I was with our lifestyle. Just ten minutes from home I held down a great paying position with lots of fringe benefits. I had a private savings account – Sylvy's Emergency Stash. Boy, I hated the thought I would no longer be able to feed it. I rarely had occasion to use any of the money, or the need, but, it sure was nice to know it was there. My husband was aware of the account, but often teased me about the amount. I never told him, it was our little game.

I love my husband dearly, we've shared a good life together, ups and downs. No one surpasses his sense of humor. I often tease him that I married him only because he kept me laughing.

For better or worse, in sickness and in health, but, oh! God! Where in the marriage contract does it say for 24 hours a day, 7 days a week, 365 days a year?

We talked more and some more. Made our plans, put our house on the market.

I lived on tranquillizers during the invasion of our privacy by prospects and suspects.

Early one afternoon, just as I arrived home, the key still in the lock, the phone was ringing.

"Hello, this is Mr. Rae, from the Rae-O Realty. I would like to bring a client over to see your house, let's say about 3 P.M. They've seen it before, like it, but want to take another look."

"What time is it now? 1:30 P.M. Great, fine, come on over."

"This will give me time to make sure the place is in order," I talked to myself.

I put on the stereo, for atmosphere, soft soothing music. Oops, no sound, turned on the light switch, no lights. Ran down to the basement to check the circuit breakers. All in the proper position, can't take any chances, I checked each one anyway, pushed the levers up and down, maybe one was stuck. Nope, nothing wrong. Called my next door neighbors, they had lights. I could not reach my husband on the phone.

"What now Sylvy? Don't panic," again talking to myself. "Think! Think! I don't want to blow this, a good prospect, their second visit."

I pulled out the phone book, called an electrical outfit in the area, told them my tale of woe.

They were sympathetic, a truck was due back any minute, they will send it right over.

It was getting close to 2 P.M. With a sigh of relief, I saw the truck pull into the driveway about 2:30 P.M. The important electrical elements were checked, but, the problem could not be located.

Talking with the electrician at the circuit breaker box, I suddenly remembered.

About noon, just before I left the house, I was in the basement and noticed a wire hanging loose. I pushed it onto the shelf and went out.

The electrician checked the wire and discovered it had been shorted. When I had pushed the wire onto the shelf, it hit an exposed wire, causing the shortage.

"Gosh! Thank God you found the trouble. How long will it take to fix?"

"Fifteen minutes, maybe a half hour the most."

"Oh great!"

Knock! Knock! "Darn, why does Mr. Rae have to be so punctual?"

An electrician's truck in my driveway, no lights in my house. A hot prospect to purchase my house at my door. "Sorry, my electric system blew. Come back tomorrow." I could just see the deal going down the drain.

No way!

"Good afternoon! Come right in. I hope you will bear with me for just a minute or two. I'm having the electrical system checked out, and the lights have to be off for a short time. I want to make sure all is in order for the new owner." Happy that my brain went to work for me.

No sooner were the words out of my mouth the lights came back on.

"Mr. Rae, I'll leave you to your client, nice meeting you."

I excused myself and retreated to the basement.

I had to restrain myself from hugging the electrician. So what is another tranquillizer more or less? (P.S. They did not buy the house.)

While talking to a realtor, on the phone in the bedroom, I sat down on the edge of the bed.

"May I bring over a client in a short while? We are just a few blocks away."

"Sure, happy to have them come."

"See you within the hour." He hung up.

Just as I put down the receiver, my son joined me in the bedroom.

"Hi, Mom! Stopped by to say hello." He plopped down next to me, the bed collapsed and the leg snapped off.

"Look what you did!" I scolded. "A realtor is bringing over a client in a little while. What do we do now?"

"Slow down, Mom! Take a deep breath, keep the faith."

He ran down the stairs and into the garage, minutes later returned to the bedroom with three red bricks. He held up the corner of the bed while I slipped them in place.

"Voilà, perfect," he assured me. "Mom, with the bedspread on no one could tell the bed has a broken wooden leg." It took a split second for the pun to sink in.

"Very funny, very funny." We had a good laugh. His mission

accomplished, he calmed me down. I thanked him, kissed him and threw him out.

The bricks remained there until we sold the bedroom set. (P.S. This client bought the house.)

One evening at dinner, I asked, "Bernie, would you by chance, know the name of the best magician in the world?"

"Why do you want to know that?"

"Because it is going to take a magician to help us."

"Help us with what?"

"Help us fit an accumulation of an eight-room house, garage, storage room and basement, into a two bedroom condo."

Bernie answered as husbands have through the ages. He shrugged.

We gave our children what pieces they wanted, and, we were happy in the knowledge some of our collectibles were remaining in the family.

Then, one evening, while cleaning out a storage closet, we came across scrapbooks and photo albums, some dating back to our engagement. Also there were letters and post cards our boys had sent to us from summer camp, twenty or twenty-five years ago.

As we sat on the floor sorting out what to take, we read the children's mail. It was so funny, we got hysterical laughing. Then we started to cry. There we were, two grown people, hugging each other, rolling on the floor in laughter and tears, turning the pages of life, walking into unknown chapters.

## Generational Humor

In my nine-year-old grandchild's science class, the subject for the day was *hibernation*. The teacher asked: "Does anyone know into what state of inactivity animals go during winter months?"

My nine-year-old grandchild answered, *"Florida."*

Golf Course Chatter

# Kitchen know! No! No!

Living in this vacation wonderland, I automatically followed the lifestyle of my previous vacations instead of that of a resident.

Our evenings were reserved for the social whirl of visiting friends, dinner out every night, breakfast and lunch ditto, theatre shows, taking in all events, home only to shower and change clothes.

Heaven forbid! I didn't sun worship at the pool or beach every day as I did when a vacationer.

I blocked out the fact that I'm living here now as a permanent resident, and do not have to rush helter and skelter to take everything in before my vacation is over. Heck! This is the life, I am having a great time, complete freedom of day-to-day responsibilities.

Several weeks of this, until one afternoon my husband said, "Listen, my dear, we have to talk, when you find time from your busy schedule. Slow down and make an appointment with me."

"Ha! Ha! I'm all ears, how about right now, my love?"

A serious expression crossed his face. He answered, "I have two off-limit words to say to you – food-shopping."

"Okay, if you are hungry, I'll make our dinner reservations for an earlier hour tonight. That takes care of food. Now, what kind of shopping do you want to do? Clothes, pants, socks, bathing suit, what—?"

"Just wait a minute, slow down, hold it, I mean shopping for food. I think it is about time you started to use the kitchen," he retorted.

"I bought you a present." The card read "Remember How." It was a cook book.

"Heh there, my funny man, I think you are trying to tell me something."

My husband put his arm around me. "Wifey, in the several weeks since we made this our permanent home you haven't cooked home once – and—"

"Remember, before we got married, I told you the kitchen wasn't my favorite room in the house?"

He threw back, "And all through our marriage you proved it."

"Now, listen, just a minute, wise-guy, you and the kids survived, and turned out none the worse for it. I came through like a trooper, when I had to. Besides, when we talked, or you talked, about retirement, you promised we would be on a permanent vacation in the south. Okay, literally or figuratively, whatever. You set me up. What a sneaky way to get me to leave the north!" I proclaimed: "Now you tell me vacation time is over."

"Yup! That's what I'm telling you."

I told my husband, "I wondered how long it would take you to put the skids under me. Can't hate a gal for trying."

I'm not going back up north to be home. It was time to kick the vacation illusion out the front door and take on the responsibility of maintaining my permanent home as I had done before the southern exodus.

I gave my husband a big kiss and hug and thanked him for being so cooperative, compassionate and understanding. A real doll, that is why I married him.

Deep down inside me, I keep hoping a scientist would invent a nourishment pill, taken in the morning, to replace eating the rest of the day. So, I wouldn't have to food shop or cook, no kitchen duties.

I love you!

## Condo One-liners!

"Being of sound mind – I'm spending my money as fast as I can."

"I want to live long enough to be a problem to my children."

"Everyone living in this condo brings happiness. Some by moving in; some by moving out."

"If a man thinks for one minute that he understands women, he has it timed just right."

# Body Beautiful – When?

If Noah Webster was alive today and cognizant of the senior citizen condo retirement lifestyle, he would revise the definition of retirement in his dictionary.

Mr. Webster's New World Dictionary of the American Language defines retirement: "withdrawal-privacy." Condo-ville defines retirement: "involvement-fishbowl." I did not start out that way.

At first, I enjoyed a three-mile walk in the calm, clear, serenity of the morning. I liked to get out there before the good air was used up at 7 A.M.

A healthy steady pace, arms swinging, every part of my body reaping the benefits; with proper protection against the tropical sun, conspicuous sunglasses, large floppy hat, stereo transistor attached to my belt, ear pieces in place, the antenna flying in the wind, I would get all the acid out of my system. Stomach in, shoulders straight.

When I completed that walk every morning, my mind and body were ready for anything.

Then, one day, about 7:30 A.M., a man came toward me on the walking path.

"Good morning, lovely lady." I smiled, returned the greeting and continued past him.

He turned around and called back, "It's a pleasure to see a lovely smiling face so early in the morning," came toward me and gave me a hug.

Somewhat surprised, I muttered, "Thank you," pulled away and continued my walk.

My ego hit the sky and remained there all day.

I cut my walk short to get home quickly and tell my husband about my admirer.

His immediate answer was, "Dear, you are right. I should start an exercise program. I'm going to start by walking with you." (Why did I not think of this admirer a bit sooner? My husband would no longer be called pot-belly Bernie.)

I often saw "The Hugger" on the walking path, greeting other women with a hug. Once Bernie started walking with me, I was, it seems, verboten.

On the condo itinerary was Class Registration for the new condo recreation season.

I asked myself, "Let me see, will it be aerobics, slimnastics, or aquacise?" I looked in on some of the classes in progress, just to see what it was all about. Men, women, tall, short, thin, fat. I admired their spirit. I decided to join the Aquacise class, Tuesday and Wednesday at 10:30 A.M.

I figured between my walking and swimming I would burn up a load of calories. Not true. My active morning stimulated my appetite for a sumptuous lunch. Net caloric loss "0".

My new afternoon schedule called for line dancing, lessons, two afternoons a week, Monday and Friday, 2 to 3 P.M.

Other afternoons I managed to get to the pool for sun and R and R (rest and relaxation). Just to think happy thoughts and socialize. I started a conversation.

"Hi, there. I'm from building #3" (In condo living, you are best known by your building, before your name.) "Sylvy is the name."

"Hello, I'm building #2, Clara is the name."

"So, we're neighbors. Where do you hail from?" I continued.

Condo dwellers are not Florida natives.

Clara told me. "I was born and lived in New Jersey until I married and moved to Philadelphia."

"What a coincidence!" I replied. I'm from New Jersey, born in Newark, but lived most of my married life in Maplewood."

Clara responded, "Heh! Strange world. I too was born in Newark, went to Weequahic High School, graduated in June 1937."

"Oh my gosh, I went to Weequahic High School too!

And graduated in the fall of 1937. (back in those days there was a January and June graduation.)

We spent the afternoon reminiscing about good old New Jersey. Do we miss it? The change is traumatic.

The invariable question among wives. "How do you handle your husband's retirement?"

"Clara, how about you and I sign up for the Senior Olympics?"

# Recycled Senior Citizen

Hidden in every adult is a child who wants to play!

Whistle! Whistle!

"For all participants of the Green Palm Camp Senior Olympics. The event of the year. We will be competing against three other condos. Training will start as soon as you have selected your sport." So says the athletic director.

He shouted, "Ladies and gentlemen, you all are about to become celebrities."

The director whips up the team's spirit, physically and mentally. Prodding us along, day in and day out, reassuring us the aches and pains are temporary.

We convince ourselves we're having a lot of fun and repeat the mantra, "I wouldn't worry, the aches and pains will go away, the aches and pains will go away." As the days become weeks and the weaks become dazed, under the supervision of the physical fitness director, the squads dwindle down to a precious few.

I did not make the Olympic team but I was given the honor of running (walking) with the torch.

This event turned back the calendar for me to the days of

watching our children participate in the Color Wars at their summer camp. Only this time our visiting children were cheering me and my team.

We came in third.

# Quips and Quirps

Jack to Bob!

"Boy! Am I in trouble. This togetherness is driving me nuts! My wife talks so much, I pretend not to hear her. But I blew it. She made an appointment to have my hearing tested."

Sophie to Leona!

"Carole is so conceited, the way she struts around here. If her arms were long enough, she'd be constantly hugging herself."

Fred to Herb!

"I have a part-time job in the morning and do volunteer work in the afternoon. I make sure I don't get home before 5 P.M. It makes me feel productive and useful, like when I worked. Young at heart."

# The Moped Dream

At retirement age, old dreams begin to surface. After all, if not now, when?

A few months after we settled into condo-ville, a neighbor, Danny, bought a moped bike.

This brought to surface a secret desire lying dormant within me.

Getting ready for bed, I reminded my husband about a conversation we had about ten or fifteen years ago. "Bernie, remember when the motor-cycle trend was the rage?"

"Yeah! What about it?"

"Remember your friend, Jerry Synn?" I asked.

"His sister and brother-in-law belonged to a Senior Citizen Motor Cycle Club. They traveled around the country in a group of about twenty motor-cycles, husbands and wives. When they returned, they told us it was a thrill of a lifetime."

"So, I remember the crazies."

"I told you some day when we retire, I'd love to own a motor-cycle, not just a single one but one that has a side-car attached."

He sat up in bed, looked at me for a second, "Oh, of course, sure, okay," he humored me. "Turn off the light, go to sleep. You have had a busy day, with all your involvements. We'll talk some more tomorrow. Goodnight."

"Dear, do you know Danny's wife Mimi?" If you don't you will. Danny rides the moped to the tennis courts in the morning. Sometimes I see his bike at the driving range. I know it is his because he has an American flag attached to his antenna."

"What do you mean, I will know his wife?"

"You will know it is Mimi, Danny's wife, when you see her on the bike with an American flag. She rides the moped to the local supermarket. I see her come home with the shopping bags in the basket."

There's no answer from Bernie. I think he has fallen asleep, so I do too. I dream I'm driving a motorcycle with a side-car, scooting around town, helmet snapped in place, no leather jacket (too warm).

At breakfast, I begin: "It will be fun and I promise to drive it only locally."

"Hold it! Drive what locally?"

"The motorcycle with the side-car. It will be great for daytime chores, the library, market, movies, it will get into a little parking space. What a gas saver, save wear and tear on our car. The gas guzzler. I'll drive, you be the passenger."

"You trying to get us killed?" Bernie shouted. "Listen," I said, "the side-car has three wheels."

He raved, "Three wheels isn't going to make it less dangerous than two wheels. The idea is crazy and so are you."

He saw he'd taken the air out of me, so his tone became conciliatory. He continued, "I will agree to sit in the side-car if it is secured by a minimum of three seat belts, a hard hat and a double scotch and soda."

"I jumped up out of my chair, yelled, "It's a deal." Hugged and kissed him.

I'm still shopping around for that vehicle.

My husband is ecstatic in the thought that they are not easy to come by.

Twice as much husband isn't too much. Is it?

## Age Knows no Bounds!

As I sit here pool-side with my peers, it's a nice feeling to know that now... I belong to the FBI (Female Body Inspector).

Anonymous

# Goldfish Bowl

At about four or five years of age, give or take a year or two, my sons, like all kids, had a bowl of goldfish. As I fed them, (the kids never fed their pets.) I'd wonder if, and what, they thought about the odd looking creature glaring down at them.

Perhaps they thought, Hey, you out there, give me my food and get lost. I got my spouse here and I want my privacy.

Today living in condo-ville, I feel like those fish. When Bernie and I go to and from our condo, very often with our arms around each other, our fellow condo dwellers observe us. After a few weeks of this observation, a neighbor, Phil, approached Bernie, "Hey, Bernie, you cannot be a member of our Men's Club at our condo because you are simply too darn nice to your wife. It doesn't look right for the rest of the guys. So, if you don't cut it out, we'll send the hit squad up to see you, and straighten you out once and for all."

It was all done in good humor, but it emphasized our lack of privacy in as simple a matter as walking out to the car, or a show of affection.

Another time we were invited to an anniversary party about fifty miles out of town. Having a grand time, we made no effort to leave the affair early. We arrived home about 1:30 A.M.

The following morning, as I returned from my exercise class, I met Julius from the next building. Julius was nick-named, "the eye," and I was soon to discover why.

"Where were you and Bernie until 1:30 A.M.?" He had taken me by surprise, I was about to answer him with, "What's it your business?" But, mentally counted to ten and replied,

"How do you know?"

"I was out for some air, and I checked all the cars. Everyone was parked but yours."

"Thank you for your concern, Julius, (I was about to say 'the eye'), much appreciated," I muttered. I guess his intentions were good.

There was a time I stuck my nose into a neighbor's business.

Herman and his wife are snowbirds. From the day they arrive until the day they leave, four or sometimes five months later, he likes to run out for breakfast by himself every morning, at 7:00 or 7:30 A.M.

One Thanksgiving morning, I saw him drive away just as I started my walk. He was back in minutes, passing me on the road. Thinking something was wrong, I approached him as he got out of his car. "Herman, are you okay?"

He replied, "Sure, but damn it, the darn restaurant is closed for the holiday and now I have to have breakfast with my old windbag wife."

I said, "Why don't you go inside, tell Bertha you decided to come home and have breakfast with her because she is the greatest and you want to spend the holiday with her."

He laughed, looked me straight in the eye, and said, "She is too smart to fall for that baloney."

The pièce de resistance of condo fishbowl living; I had taken myself a part-time office job, leaving my condo about 8:00 A.M. on Wednesday and Friday.

This particular week I switched a Friday to a Thursday. On Friday morning about 8:00 I went into the club house to check the activities for the following week.

The maintenance man saw me and shouted, "Madam, You better get going, you will be late for your job this Friday morning."

I turned to him in surprise. "Richard, it is okay, I'm not working today, I switched to Thursday this week. But, how did you know I go to work?"

"Oh, madam, everybody knows."

"Thanks Richard, I appreciate your concern."

All condo residents are kept abreast of communal happenings by checking the strategically placed bulletin board – meetings, policy decisions, all daily events, plus letters placed in the wrong mail box.

The mail area ought to be roped off from the onslaught of the building occupants, for the protection of the mail carrier. He/she is so over burdened, especially during "season", it is understandable when a mistake is made and a letter is thrown into the box of another resident. My husband and I left early the day a letter arrived for me from a publicity agency. In error, it was put in the box of our condo captain.

By the time we returned home, in the early evening, most neighbors knew I received a letter from a publicity agency. They had seen the envelope on the bulletin board, placed there by the condo captain.

Some neighbors couldn't restrain their curiosity and questioned my need for a publicity agent.

I whispered, jokingly, to Marge, Jane and Sara, "I'm a spy for a condo scandal sheet, let me know if you hear any gossip."

A few days later, I received an anonymous letter, with wildly fictional stories about Marge, Jane and Sara. My joke had back-fired. I confessed to the gals, "The letter I received from the publicity agency was from a girlfriend who works for a public relations agency."

Solution: If I need mail privacy I'll get myself a P.O. box number.

"Mr. Webster – wherefore art thou?"

# The Refrigerator Light Never Goes Off

We retired southern belt condo-ville dwellers have to condition ourselves when it comes to guests, be it our children, grandchildren, friends, or invited or uninvited guests. "Yeah! We are in the neighborhood, mind if we stop by for a few days?

"What is your name?"

Beware!

We handled our first attempt at entertaining overnight holiday guests quite well, with the cooperation of my twice as much husband. Especially since they stayed ten nights. It was our first Christmas-New Year's holiday at our two-bedroom, two-bath condo.

Our son Rob and his wife, who live in Minnesota, were flying to upstate New York to visit her parents over Christmas, then down to us over New Year's.

Our single son Neil was flying down from New York City. Rob's two single sisters-in-law were flying to upstate New York.

I suggested to my husband:

"What do you think of the idea of inviting all of Rob's in-laws down here for the combined holidays? None of them has ever been to Florida."

Bernie gasped, "What! Are you nuts? You are biting off more than you can chew!"

I continued, "Instead of Rob, his wife, Neil and the girls all flying in different directions, they will all meet here."

"Syl, you are friends with the in-laws now, do you want to be enemies?"

"Dear, have faith! Have faith! It's a blending of families, it will work fine." I kept telling myself.

"Where will you put them? What will you do with them for all that time? How do you intend to entertain them?" The more I contemplated, and the more Bernie painted out the negatives, the more challenging it became. And to me, a challenge is a commandment.

"Heh! we'll rough it. I know Rob's mother-in-law is very formal, but, this will be a very informal, no fussing, nothing special, do-as-you want vacation!"

"I'll keep the refrigerator and freezer stacked; everyone will feel free to come and go as they please, sleep as late as they want, eat whenever they want, serve themselves. It could be a lot of fun."

"What about the sleeping arrangements?" Bernie, the ever practical one, inquired.

"First of all, I think we should give the senior in-laws our bedroom. Rob and his wife the small bedroom. The girls we'll set up on folding cots in the corner of the living room, Neil in a sleeping bag in the corner of the dining room."

I laughed heartily, "Welcome to the Sylvy's dormitory."

"You forgot someone." Bernie put in as I paused for breath.

"Who?" I asked.

"Us"

"Oh, I forgot to tell you. We can sleep at my sister's house every night. Since she lives in the next court, no problem. I've already talked to her about it… have no fear, the favor will be returned."

"That's what I am afraid of," he retorted: "Wait a minute, wifey, you spoke to your sister about this plan of yours and now you ask me what I think."

"Oops! I plead guilty. Come to bed. I'll make it up to you."

"I'll empty a couple of drawers for them." I said, "and make space in the closet. The kids have plenty of drawer space in the dresser. Neil will share drawers. The girls can live out of their luggage."

"You made up your mind to go ahead with this crazy plan. I hope you don't rue the day. What the hell, go have your fun. Full speed ahead. Lady overboard."

I called Rob, threw the idea at him, he loved it, called Mim, his mother-in-law, extended the invitation. "We deeply appreciate your thoughtfulness. It will be too much for you and Bernie," she argued, "taking advantage of your generosity."

"Nonsense," I argued back. "If we didn't want you all with us we wouldn't have extended our invitation. Come on, let your hair down, speak to your guy and the girls. We are going to have a holiday to remember."

About four days later she called to say "we accept." Male and female pitched in, selecting the chores of their choice.

We, the host and hostess weren't allowed to wash a dish, or serve. They treated us as their guests! Everyone was stupendous, the refrigerator light never went off. My trips to the food market were so frequent, my car found its own way.

At the five o'clock happy hour, we gathered, all talking at the same time, enjoying the closeness, and I mean closeness! The vacation ended with a gala New Year's Eve party in our living room, for about thirty people. People came to see if we were still talking with each other.

After everyone's departure, Bernie and I moved back into our own bedroom, our own bed, our own condo. Suddenly, with everyone gone, it seemed huge, and lonely.

"Good-night, sweetheart, little lady is always right. Thank you for a grand and glorious holiday. Happy New Year!"

# *The Host and Hostess Credo*

1. I accept the tumult.
2. I accept open luggage in every room.
3. I accept the beds never being made.
4. I accept their staying out all hours.
5. I accept the dishes in the sink all day.
6. I accept the open dresser drawers.
7. I accept the half closed closet doors.
8. I accept wet bathing suits and towels hanging in the bathroom and over chairs.
9. I accept the newspapers and magazines all over the house.
10. I accept the refrigerator light never going off.

I love company!

# Retirement Shopping

"Driving bargains."

I'm getting used to the fact that, like God, my husband is always around.

"Sylvy, come here, hurry, I want you to see something on television."

"Can't now, I'm in the bathroom."

"Sylvy, where is the TV Guide?"

"You are sitting on it."

"Sylvy, where are my glasses?"

"On your head."

"Sylvy, the telephone is ringing."

"So, answer it."

"Sylvy, where did you put the… why… when… where…?"

Most wives complain about their husbands going supermarket shopping with them. I did not anticipate such a problem as I could never get my husband near a supermarket, let alone into one.

Now, upon retirement, he began keeping a running shopping list and clipping coupons out of the Sunday papers. Now he was named 'The Sunday Coupon Clipper'.

By now, I'm not surprised when he asks: "Do you want me to go shopping with you today?"

"I'm not going marketing today."

"I'll help. I'll help when you go."

"No thanks, I'll do okay by myself."

"But, it will be faster and easier with the two of us," he pushed. "I'll get some items and you get others."

So, he comes with me. This conversation is a ritual.

We play "put and take." He puts all the coupon items into the cart. I take most of them out of the cart and put them back on the shelf. I don't use most of the coupon items. We argue about it later, whether buying something simply because there's a coupon on it constitutes saving money.

Before retirement, Heaven forbid, I should ever have asked my husband to go shopping with me to pick out my clothes. He hated to buy clothes when he was single.

I always went with him when the time came to replace his wardrobe. He'd buy the first thing he put on and rush out of the store... I often threatened him, "Your clothes shopping antics upset me so, I'm seriously thinking of sending you off to a nudist colony."

So, it was a major life change, about nine o'clock one beautiful cool morning, when I had decided I was taking the day off, by myself, for myself, and I announced, "Bernie, I'm going clothes shopping, alone. Be back when I get back, four or five o'clock, maybe."

"Gee, you'll be gone that long?"

"I don't know, if I find what I want, I'll be back earlier." I'm looking for bargains. Remember, half as much money!

"Tell you what." Bernie told me what. "Suppose I go with you, I'll drive so you won't get too tired. It'll give you more energy for shopping. I'll carry the packages. Okay?"

"No thank you," I exploded.

"You know how you hate the malls and department stores. Your impatience makes me nervous. I don't enjoy myself when you are like that!"

As I was dressing, I sensed his disappointment.

He would be alone all day. So, I agreed, with conditions. "Take a book with you," I said, "find a seat, relax and read. Don't look at your watch. Don't keep asking me how much longer I'll be, or when we will be getting home. Don't tell me it is getting late."

"Great! It's a deal, Lunch is on me."

He roamed around the mall, in and out of the ladies' shops with me, he behaved himself. He actually looked as though he was enjoying himself. He carried my packages, and this did make it easier for me. I really enjoyed having him along. He did the driving. My energy level was sky high. At home later, he admitted, he'd had a good day, and enjoyed the new experience. Especially happy to see me relaxed.

Now he shops with me quite often and relaxes in the "honey do" seats with all the other husbands. What is a "honey do" seat?

When wives try on pants, dresses, sweaters, whatever, we strut out of the dressing room, over to where our husbands sit and ask, "Honey do you like this outfit?"

Togetherness… "I love you too."

The crazy drivers in condo-ville annoy the daylights out of my husband. He becomes so frustrated driving, I end up doing most of the driving, especially for marketing. This is okay with me, because, for many years, I mean many years, I drove all over. In the previous world I was the only one with a driver's license. I had a boyfriend who had his own car and taught me to drive the day I became of age. I knew where I wanted to go and how to get there, easily. Love to read maps and acquired a good sense of direction.

Today, I have a co-pilot.

"Turn in this direction."

"Go that way, go this way."

"Take this street to avoid a light."

"Take the next right turn, save two traffic lights."

"The light just turned green."

"You are coming to a red light."

"Why did you stop?"

"To let you out of this car. Do you know where I want you to go?" I shouted, "Get out of my hair, go get yourself a job. Retirement, a day of infamy!"

"For better or for worse. Do you take this man?"

Since retirement, and having to live on a fixed income, I, and many other wives, have become, well, let's euphemistically call it, "frugal".

In order to encourage business, a great many restaurants offer discounts, or what they call, early bird dinners, which means you have to eat before 5:30 P.M. Which means getting there at 4:30 to get in line.

Pre-retirement we never dined (ate supper) before eight or nine o'clock at night, depending when Bernie arrived home from work. But, when in Rome, or condo-ville, we do not refuse our friends when they ask us to join them for an early bird meal. Even though it means the whole afternoon is shot, we flap our wings and off we fly.

After a late breakfast, one day, we went about a number of errands. By mid-afternoon, we found ourselves in the area of a restaurant specializing in my husband's favorite dinner – barbecued spare ribs. The hostess informed us, "The early bird dinner starts in fifteen minutes, at 3:30 if you wait the few minutes, it will save you $3.00."

By now, conditioned to early bird thinking, I suggested, "Let's go to the bar for a before-dinner drink while we wait."

The tab at the bar was $5.50.

Math shows a net loss of $2.50 waiting for the early bird dinner.

So much for the early bird bargains.

# Organ Recital

Several husbands, indulging in social freedom they did not have when working, enjoying the comradeship of condo life, were off by themselves in their corner of the new world, under the canopy, at the far end of the pool. They were performing an "Organ Recital", which means discussing organ repairs, aches and pains. Each was trying to top the other about their recent operations.

Ben sat quietly not saying a word. After the men had all said their piece, he stood up and seriously challenged the group.

"Until recently, you fellows have had clear sailing and are now on the mend, right? I have a constant pain that has been with me for the last forty years. Since retirement it has progressed and is now with me twenty-four hours a day." He paused, looked at them and sat down.

The men glanced at each other, not a word was spoken, one gentleman finally said, "Sorry Ben, we didn't know. What is the pain and where is it?'

Ben solemnly bent in toward the center of the group and blurted out, "Yes, I have this one major pain, in the butt. What is it? My wife! Being with her twenty-four hours a day, what a pain in the butt. I'd like to ship her back to Chicago."

For a split second, there was silence, then a roar of laughter and applause.

Ben, rolled over laughing and jokingly, quipped, "Guess their smarty 'twice as much husband' jabs are beginning to back-fire. Heh guys how about a twice as much wives' club? But guess it is not easy for them. I wouldn't want me around twenty-four hours a day. Agreed men?" Unanimous!

What with orders from the urologist, that, healthwise, we should all drink, at least, eight glasses of water per day, the Fountain of Youth is constantly being tapped by retirees.

Bert, a neighbor following doctor's orders, since his prostate operation, frequently will get up during the night to answer the call of nature.

He was told by his downstairs neighbor, "Bert, I hear you in the bathroom very often, especially during the night, about three or four o'clock."

"Jeff," Bert replied, "I try not to disturb anyone during the night. So, I never flush the toilet."

"Hell no!" Jeff quickly replied. "I don't mean the flushing. I hear you tinkle!"

Bert's fast retort, "Guess your ears are better than my urinary tract."

Jennie's (Mr. Clean) husband, Abner, was in the hospital, recovering from his prostate operation.

I called Jennie to ask how Abner was progressing. "Abner is doing just fine," she reported, "but I'm not."

"What's wrong with you?" I questioned.

"He just called," she said, unhappily, "I have to pick him up within the hour, he is being discharged a day early."

"That should make you happy," I said.

"Yeah, but you don't know Abner," she countered, "He is an obsessive compulsive neatnik! I use to be able to stand it, he wasn't home all day, but, since he retired, having him test for dust twenty-four hours a day... Come on!"

"I was all set to relax, throw the dishes into the sink, and leave them there. Leave the newspapers on the floor, kick off my shoes, let then stay wherever they land, enjoy watching television without my loveable neatnik spouse on reconnaissance patrol."

We both burst out laughing. "Thank God he's all right," she giggled.

## Pesty Neighbor

A quiet evening alone with your spouse is a welcome respite in the condo-ville whirl of activities. Bernie welcomed the idea when I told him,

"Dear, believe it or not, I am not making any plans for Saturday night. Let's stay home, relax, and watch TV. There's a program I'd like to see. Goes on at eight o'clock for two hours."

The only problem was a pesky neighbor who often made impromptu uninvited visits.

So, we watched TV in the bedroom, at the back of our condo, which left the front completely dark.

During the nine o'clock commercial, I rushed into the kitchen for some ice-cream. Stupidly forgetful, I put on the kitchen light.

In a few seconds, there was a knock on the door, and there stood Pesky!

"I don't like the program my husband is watching. What do you have on your TV?" she asked.

"I don't know the name of it," I lied. "Actually, we're just enjoying the time alone, together." I emphasized *alone*.

She ignored the remark, walked past me into the kitchen and sat down.

Damn it, I thought, how can I tactfully get rid of her? My

husband saved the day, oops, night.

In his bathrobe, he sauntered into the kitchen. Then, in a very seductive tone, he whispered to Mrs. Pesky.

"Sylvy and I are about to enjoy a romantic interlude. I can't handle the two of you tonight. Call me for an appointment." He led her to the door.

By the next evening, the whole court had heard of my husband's proposition. We enjoyed the rest of the movie.

My twice as much husband is now known as the Don Juan of the geriatric set.

He no longer walks, but struts, to maintain his reputation.

# Early Show-Ups

When you're retired, every day is Sunday.

Because our time is free, retired people are always early. In fact, early – early – early. I learned this the hard way.

I had invited twenty-two guests for a buffet dinner on a Saturday night. Bernie worked with me for days – shopping, (no coupons) preparing foods, getting the house in order, running out for last minute items.

All was in proper order at 4 P.M., which left two free hours before the guests were to arrive.

I suggested that we lay down and get some much needed rest.

"No argument from me," Bernie shot back. I undressed, pushed back the bedspread.

"I'll shower after I nap. Do your want to shower now or later?" I asked.

"I'll shower now," he answered, "then the bathroom with the shower will be all yours."

"How about a scotch and soda?" he offered.

"Okay, please make it a weak one, thanks," I replied. I was sitting on the bed, sipping my drink, looking forward to the short rest.

Bernie sauntered out of the shower, at about 4:30 P.M. Suddenly, a knock on the door. He grabbed his robe and went to the door.

It was Lila and Mike, two of our guests.

"I know you won't mind our being so early," Lila gushed, seeing Bernie in his robe, explaining.

"We were visiting relatives, and they had to leave for an early dinner date, and you were so close."

Bernie got me out of the bedroom, I sat with them in my sarong-dressing gown, while Bernie dressed. When he returned, I excused myself, showered, put on my makeup, and dressed in a rush.

The other guests arrived about 5:30 P.M. This I had sort of expected, knowing the early-bird habit.

My dinner was a huge success, but the host and hostess were completely bushed.

That catnap would have helped.

In the future I decided I would invite dinner guests for 7 P.M. hoping they would not arrive before 6 P.M. Falling off to sleep, after a fast clean-up job, I said, "Dear, remember pre-retirement days up north? Our guests worked, so, they were never on time. Always late. Now, in retirement, they are never on time either way. Always early! Seems we can't win."

"Goooodnight…!"

## Wife's Lament To Husband

Please:

"Clean the toothpaste off the sink!"

"Don't clog the basin when you shave!"

"Don't splatter on the mirror!"

"Hang the towel back on the rack!"

"Use the floor mat when you come out of the shower!"


## Wife to Wife!

"I shouldn't make these demands!"

"Thank God, he is here to dirty things!"

# A Week (Weak) Stomach! Can't Take it!

Holidays! It's time for parents to unload their school-aged darlings onto the retired doting grandparents in condo-ville.

In an attempt to provide companionship for the "little ones", the first step on the agenda is for Grandma to actively circulate among friends, neighbors, poolside, in the club house, at the card games, and ask,

"Do any of you have grandsons visiting for the holidays? My twelve-year-old grandson will be here." I heard a few yeahs!

"Let's plan on getting together, arrange for places to take them." This, I planned with Martha. We'd figured they'd match.

By planning ahead, hopefully, Grandma and Grandpa will retain their sanity and all will be happy! God is kept mighty busy come holiday time. Every grandparent's thought begins with: *I pray*!

Grandma has stacked the refrigerator until the sides bulged. She cooked for a week, prior to the arrival of her twelve-year-old grandson, Michael... his favorites for each night of the week (information acquired from his mother). This left available one or two nights for eating out. Even though Grandma and Grandpa aren't crazy about going to restaurants in season, especially holiday time, when every place is crowded, they agreed, "It's Michael's vacation," they wanted him to enjoy.

On the day of his arrival, she said to her husband, "Tonight, for dinner, I'll serve Michael's favorite of favorites."

Arriving back home from the airport, Grandma settled Michael in, then, she retreated into the kitchen to warm up the dinner. As she reached for the handle of the refrigerator, she heard her husband say,

"It's a deal Michael, if it's pizza you want, pizza you get for dinner tonight."

Grandma yelled in from the kitchen.

"Michael, not tonight. I have your favorite of favorites for dinner tonight."

"Oh Grandma, please be a good gal, put it in the freezer for tomorrow. Please!"

Back into the freezer it went, and there it stayed all week.

The next day's conversation; "Grandma, I really enjoyed the Italian dinner last night. How about some Chinese tonight?"

The next night it was Southwest. The next Thai.

Rummaging through the restaurant section of the newspaper, Michael managed to come up with a Korean restaurant. During the course of the week, Grandma managed to work in one American dinner to satisfy her dietary needs. Her dessert every night: one or two spoons full of an antacid.

But it was a small price to pay to advance Michael's dream, his career (he aspires to be a chef on TV).

The "well-laid plans" of Grandma and Martha went "awry"; Michael and Martha's grandson had their own day-time plans, they disappeared till dinner time, which was not something the grandparents wished. After all, they wanted to spend more time with Michael. But as the youngsters had adventures that only their generation could follow, they managed to stray off and have fun.

As the plane carrying Michael flew from them, Grandma said, "I'm relaxed for the first time since Michael arrived!" Looks at Grandpa, takes his hand and tells him,

"I could not have survived this week without your help! Thanks for being twice as much husband."

Grandpa commented, "Michael really had a great time. He did everything he wanted. Did not hear the word "no" all the time he was here. He will surely want to come back. Let's remember to put in a good supply of antacids. We love when they come, we love when they go. "God bless them!"

They both laughed happily and content with each other.

# Grandparents Prayers

1. I pray –    They arrive safely!

2. I pray –    We do not have cold weather, so they can spend the days at the pool or the beach!

3. I pray –    It doesn't rain and they are confined to the small apartment!

4. I pray –    They stay out of trouble!

5. I pray –    They are happy with our plans!

6. I pray –    They stay healthy and safe!

7. I pray –    They stay out of the neighbors' hair!

8. I pray –    We live through the vacation!

9. I pray –    They arrive home safely!

10. I pray –   They visit their other grandparents next year!

Thank you God!

# Unretired Retiree

After a few years of retired condo life the blush fades off the rose, for some people. The issue is restlessness.

Husband and or wife may disappear from the locale of the condo action.

Abby now works three days a week in a local dress shop. Betty took a job three days a week in a posh boutique featuring designer purses.

Lottie puts in three hours a day at the local library. Sam helps out a friend in his bakery twice a week.

My husband asked Phil, "I haven't seen Hank around the past week or so. Is he all right?"

"He went out and got himself a part-time job, selling, on the road. He was a salesman, works three days a week. He answered an ad in the papers."

"What prompted that?"

"He started to get restless, didn't know whether he was getting in his own way, or his wife was bugging him about being in her way."

My husband questioned, "Is it twice as much husband or half as much money?"

Both Phil and Bernie agreed, "Busy bodies, healthy minds.

Jerry found himself a hobby, for a while anyway. He joined a fishing club, and took special lessons, twice a week. After graduation, he qualified for surf, pier and boat fishing. Jerry had learned where and when to fish to catch what kind of fish.

His wife Helen, framed the diploma and hung it in the bathroom, so that Jerry could see it every morning when he shaved.

She confided to me, "I'm free! I'm free! Free at last."

Several weeks later, she confessed, "If I never see or eat fish again, it will not be too soon. Would you believe, when Jerry brought home his first catch, he insisted that I clean them. I didn't want to discourage him, so I cleaned them but just that once."

Helen went on, "My condo smelled like a fish store. I think the reason the neighbors didn't complain was because I supplied them with fish all season."

Not only had he become a fanatic fisherman, but, Jerry then took to telling fish jokes: "What does the fisherman answer when someone wants to borrow a hundred dollars?"

Answer: "No! But, I'll give you a fin!"

Helen told me: "I was the happiest wife in condo-ville when my husband unhooked himself from the fishing club," laughing at her quip.

A short time later, Jerry discovered wood carving. "Every Wednesday afternoon he attends class," Helen reported.

"He bought himself all the proper carving tools, all expensive. And now, my home is full of miniature wooden horses, reindeer, birds, ducks and unicorns. Maybe next he will want to build an ark!"

As Helen predicted, this hobby soon whittled out. "Ouch!"

Jerry's newest venture in the hobby department is photography.

"I can't picture this," Helen punned, "The results have to be negative. Thank God for my sense of humor," she continued. "He is spending so much money. The best fishing equipment is now lying in the garage. The special wood carving knives are stored away. Now, this photography equipment. It will cost a mint."

"I'm taking bets on how long this hobby will last. Maybe I'll recoup some money on the bets."

Alice's husband, Carl, also went over the deep-end with computers.

He wondered into a computer store at the mall and came out three hours later.

"I'm going to look further, into these computers," he said. "Maybe I'll buy one."

"Not for that kind of money," Alice shouted. "Go back to work, It will serve both purposes. Less husband and more money."

Carl really knew how to convince a gal. When he gave her the reason, she couldn't refuse. "It will keep me out of your hair dear."

He set himself up a place in the spare room and put in over $2000.00 worth of equipment.

Alice told me,

"He is fascinated with the machine, he can't believe what it accomplishes. He goes into the room at ten o'clock in the morning and I don't see him until dinner time. I have to remind him about eating."

"Sounds good," I replied.

"Sometimes he gets out of bed at two o'clock in the morning, just to play with it."

Alice looked thoughtful for a moment, "I made a snotty remark to him about the expense," she confessed. "If your computer friend is capable of programming so many wonders. Get it to program a way of getting back your $2000 plus."

Although Helen and Alice don't have twice as much husband around because of the hobbies, they do have less than half as much money, because of the cost of those hobbies. The nearness of you!

Why not?

# The Battle of the Ages

"Wives are lucky to have us retired husbands around, whether they admit it or not. So we get in their hair once in awhile. So we are their shadow, some of the time. So we step on their toes whenever they turn around. But, they must admit, we do come in handy, take over and pitch in when they yell for help!"

So spoke my cousin Milt!

"My daughter Tina called and asked if we would like to have our grandson Elliott visit during his school break. Her in-laws are taking care of the baby while Tina and her husband take off on a ski trip for a week."

Milt told his daughter:

"I don't know why he wants to visit with us. He was bored silly the last time. What in the hell are we going to do with him this trip? Besides, your mom has her bridge tournament that same week." Milt continued,

"Wait just a minute! I just got an idea. Ask him if he would like to go to Disney World! Just us two men. Mom wouldn't mind, we were there with our condo group. Us guys will rough it. I'd like to get back there myself, see some of the attractions I missed."

His wife was thrilled with the idea. She will not miss the tournament, thanks to her Milty.

"After you return from Disney World, there will be plenty time for me to spend with our precocious ten-year-old grandson," she said.

Elliott arrived on Sunday afternoon. Bright and early Monday morning they kissed Grandma good-bye. "Have a great game, hope you win the tournament. Enjoy! Take care and be sure you lock yourself in securely. I'll call you later this evening. See you in three days."

"Bye," Grandma shouted back. "Take care of each other. Drive carefully! Have a great time!'

Milt continued his tale:

"About noon we checked in at the hotel. Lost no time getting to Disney World. I bought tickets for the works. First thing – a Mickey Mouse T-shirt for Elliott, to help him get into the swing of things. He dismissed this as kids' stuff."

"I was thrilled when he asked if he could select the attractions that most appealed to him for each day. I was going to suggest he do that anyway, but, I was happy that he wanted to make the selections. Great! His enthusiasm is showing."

"His first choice was in 'Tomorrowland', you take a 'Mission to Mars' and fly around the world as if you have wings and blast off to the stars inside 'Space Mountain'. Then you glide above land, aboard the 'Wedway People Mover'. "We steamed down the 'Rivers of America' in the 'Liberty Square' riverboat, then disembarked for the

'Hall of Presidents'. There we had an audience with all our presidents, especially appealing was Abraham Lincoln."

"Elliott explained the audio electronics to me as though he was the inventor. I knew it, my grandson is a genius!"

"After a good meal at a restaurant of Elliott's choice, we headed back to the hotel for a good night's sleep."

"Early the next morning, after a delicious breakfast, back we went to Disney World. We hugged and laughed on the 'Big Thunder Mountain Runaway Railroad'. The 'Pirates of the Caribbean' wasn't one of his favorite attractions.

Milt went on:

"Around lunchtime I noticed Elliott lacked the enthusiasm of the previous day, I was having a ball and didn't mind the brief waiting in line. Thinking he was over-stimulated or whatever. (What do grandpas know about these things?) I slowed down our pace.

"Waiting in line to get into the 'Fantasyland' attraction, Elliott exclaimed: 'I'm tired Grandpa, I sure have had it, the rest of this is kids' stuff. Why don't we go back to the hotel, sit at the pool, relax for a couple of hours, have a nice dinner and watch TV?'"

"I looked at the boy astounded, 'Heh kid,' I snapped, 'which one of us is the Grandpa, you or me? You are suppose to be enjoying this and I'm suppose to complain about being tired and wanting to relax.'"

Milt fired back:

"I'm not ready to call it a day. It cost a pretty buck to come here. You're going to stay and enjoy it if it kills you!"

There was a round of applause from the line and cheers, 'Hear! Hear!' They could not help but overhear his outburst. They agreed with me whole heartedly.

"About an hour later, I decided it was useless to force the boy to stay. I drove back to the hotel, not for R and R, (rest and relaxation) but to check out and head home."

"We arrived about midnight. When my wife heard the key in the door, she jumped out of bed, shocked to see us. I assured her nothing was wrong and explained why we were home a day earlier than expected. Her grandson instituted a roll-switch. He played the old man, I enjoyed the youngster part, as a ten-year-old should."

As Elliott got on the plane to return home, Grandpa said to Grandma, "The next time our ten-year-old grandson, going on forty, visits us, I hope enough years have gone by that he is on his honeymoon."

To herself, Grandma thought, Milt is always there for me and wisely helps me out of some pretty tight spots. Thank God for him. I'm a lucky gal!

# Russian Comrade Gleeful Grandma

The more things change – the more they remain the same!

Thirty or thirty-five years ago, we lived in a newly developed suburban Shan-gri-la, a perfect atmosphere to raise children. Hopes for the future, the world is our oyster.

An afternoon highlight, a four-gal coffee klotsch, while waiting for the three o'clock school bus, when all hell breaks loose, kids running in all directions.

The A-1 topic of discussion – the neighborhood divorcees! Each gal knowing (hoping). "It isn't my husband keeping the Shan-gri-la divorcee happy!"

Thirty or thirty-five years later, an afternoon highlight, in condo-ville, four gals play bridge with Rhonda, a divorcee.

About four o'clock one afternoon, Rhonda casually announced, "I must leave by 4:30 P.M. A Russian gives me great pleasure just before dinner." She left the statement at that and walked out of the room.

We looked at each other, silence – four minds but with a single thought – each gal knowing (hoping). "It isn't my husband keeping the condo-ville divorcee happy."

Make sure our husbands are accounted for in the late afternoon. our in-laws all migrated from Russia! The nature of the beast being such, my curiosity reached its peak about two weeks later. As my divorcee friend prepared to leave I counted to ten and calmly asked, "Rhonda, when are we going to meet your Russian friend?"

For a split second a puzzled look crossed her face, suddenly she burst out laughing, hysterically. Once she regained her composure, she exclaimed, "My Russian is a cocktail, the doctor said a drink before dinner will relax me. I enjoy the taste."

"A Black Russian is made with Kahlua, which is a liqueur, with vodka, add cream or milk and you have a White Russian. Haven't you gals ever heard of it?"

We had but our suspicious minds were working overtime.

"I apologize, on behalf of all of us," I told her.

"You gals thought I had a lover? I live with four men!" "Rhonda confessed. "I go to bed with Ben-Gay! I get up with Charlie-Horse! Have lunch with Arthur-Ritus! and spend the rest of the day with Will-Power!"

There, but for the Grace of God, go I!

A perfect re-creation of something old but up dated for the present.

A few short years ago (but, it was longer) we felt so morally right, because, marriage license and the wedding ring were all due, in proper order. We felt quite smug in frowning and shaking our head as we heard of daughters moving in with boyfriends, without the benefit of clergy. My friend, Cyd, an attractive widow, admits to having a steady beau. Very often his car is parked in her driveway and remains there into the wee hours of the morning.

Cyd's visiting granddaughter, who has just become a teenager, aware of the nocturnal jaunts of grandma's friend, questioned her in my presence. "Grandma, are you shacked up with this guy?" Grandma, embarrassed, her checks did redden a bit, with humor, smiled, gave the youngster a hug and said, "My darling, at my age I want to live, love and enjoy every moment. Your grandpa is looking over us and he understands. It is wonderful to know sexuality doesn't have age limits. It is perfectly normal and healthy to have sexual desires. Love is not just for the young. We should stay active and involved."

As the song goes:

> Even though your hair has turned to silver
> and you have songs left unsung.
> Just remember, love is for everyone,
> It isn't just for the young.
> Those past sixty are grown-ups
> just growing younger!

19455149R00050

Made in the USA
San Bernardino, CA
26 February 2015